It's Not Catching

Cuts & Grazes

Heinemann
LIBRARY

Angela Royston

www.heinemann.co.uk/library
Visit our website to find out more information about **Heinemann Library** books.

To order:
 Phone 44 (0) 1865 888066
 Send a fax to 44 (0) 1865 314091   425020
💻 Visit the Heinemann Bookshop at www.heinemann.co.uk/library to browse our catalogue and order online.

First published in Great Britain by Heinemann Library, Halley Court, Jordan Hill, Oxford OX2 8EJ, part of Harcourt Education. Heinemann is a registered trademark of Harcourt Education Ltd.

Editorial: Sarah Eason and Kathy Peltan
Design: Dave Oakley, Arnos Design
Picture Research: Helen Reilly, Arnos Design
Artwork: Tower Designs UK Ltd
Production: Edward Moore

Originated by Dot Gradations Ltd.
Printed and bound in Hong Kong and China by South China Printing Company

The paper used to print this book comes from sustainable sources.

ISBN 0 431 02144 9 (hardback)
08 07 06 05 04
10 9 8 7 6 5 4 3 2 1

ISBN 0 431 02153 8 (paperback)
09 08 07 06 05
10 9 8 7 6 5 4 3 2 1

British Library Cataloguing in Publication Data
Royston, Angela
Cuts and grazes. – (It's not catching)
617.1'43

A full catalogue record for this book is available from the British Library.

Acknowledgements
The publishers would like to thank the following for permission to reproduce photographs: Alamy/Image100 p. **11**; Alamy/Peter Mumford p. **7**; Corbis p. **4**; Cumulus/David Walker p. **29**; Getty Images/Photdisc/Cole Group/Marshall Gordon p. **13**; Phillip James Photography pp. **9**, **10**, **12**, **16**, **17**, **18**, **21**, **26**, **28**; SPL p. **6**; SPL/Chris Priest p. **22**; SPL/Mark Clarke p. **5**; The Wellcome Trust pp. **25**, **27**; Trevor Clifford pp. **8**, **19**, **20**, **23**.

Cover photograph reproduced by permission of Tudor Photography.

The publishers would like to thank David Wright for his assistance in the preparation of this book.

Every effort has been made to contact copyright holders of any material reproduced in this book. Any omissions will be rectified in subsequent printings if notice is given to the publishers.

Contents

Words written in bold, **like this**, are explained
in the Glossary.

What are cuts and grazes?

Skin covers your whole body. It protects the inside of your body from the world outside. It stops dirt and **germs** getting into your body.

Sometimes something scratches or cuts into the skin. A **graze** is a shallow break in the skin, and a cut is deeper. When the skin is broken, blood leaks out and germs can get in.

Who gets cuts and grazes?

Cuts and **grazes** are not catching, but everyone cuts or grazes their skin by **accident** sometimes. Young children are unsteady on their feet and often fall over.

Older children often cut or graze themselves too. It is easy to lose your **balance** when you are skateboarding or riding a bicycle.

Scratches

Sharp things can catch and scratch your skin. Many plants, such as **brambles**, roses and **cacti** have sharp thorns. **Holly** has sharp points on its leaves.

Other sharp things can scratch you, too.
A cat has sharp claws that can break your
skin. A nail has a sharp end that can scratch.

Falls and knocks

Falling on rough ground often causes **grazes**. Stones on the ground rub off some of your skin. If you fall on something sharp, you will cut yourself.

The faster you are moving, the harder you hit the ground when you fall. This makes it more likely that you will cut or graze yourself.

Sharp tools

Scissors, knives and **razors** all have sharp edges. The sharp edges are used to cut different kinds of things, such as fabric, food, hair and plants.

Sharp tools are dangerous. Unless the person using them is very careful, the sharp tool can easily slip and cut the person's skin by **accident**.

When the skin is broken

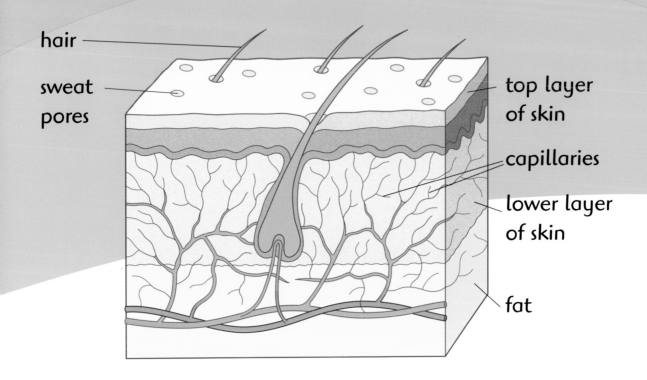

hair

sweat pores

top layer of skin

capillaries

lower layer of skin

fat

Skin is a thin layer that covers your **flesh**. The skin and the flesh below are fed by blood. The blood flows through millions of fine tubes called **capillaries**.

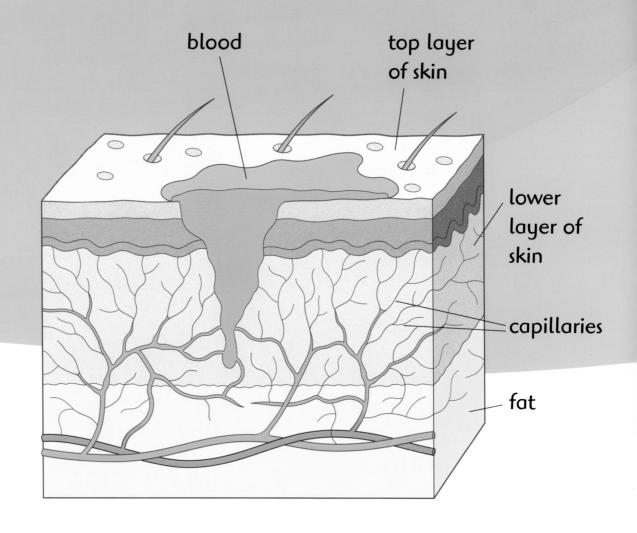

blood

top layer of skin

lower layer of skin

capillaries

fat

When your skin is **grazed** or cut, the injury usually damages some capillaries too. Blood then leaks from the capillaries and flows out of the **wound**.

Treating a graze or cut

It is important to stop dirt and **germs** from getting in through a **wound**. Wash the cut or **graze** with clean water or with a clean, wet cloth.

Sometimes you need to put **antiseptic cream** on the cut. It helps to kill germs. Do not touch other people's blood, because blood can carry germs.

stopping the bleeding

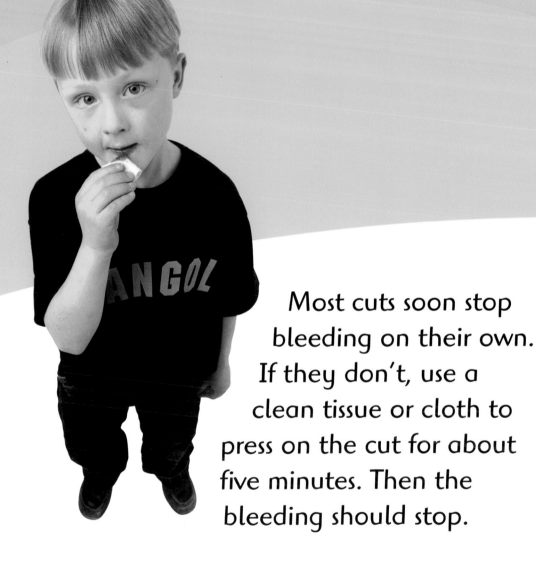

Most cuts soon stop bleeding on their own. If they don't, use a clean tissue or cloth to press on the cut for about five minutes. Then the bleeding should stop.

If a cut is very deep, you will need to get help straightaway. An adult may use a **dressing** and a **bandage** to stop the bleeding while they take you to hospital.

Plasters

You need to cover an open **wound** to stop dirt or **germs** from getting into it. A **plaster** is the best way to cover a small cut or **graze**.

If the graze is too big for a plaster, you can use a **bandage** instead. An adult will put a clean **dressing** over the wound and wind the bandage around to hold it in place.

Stitches

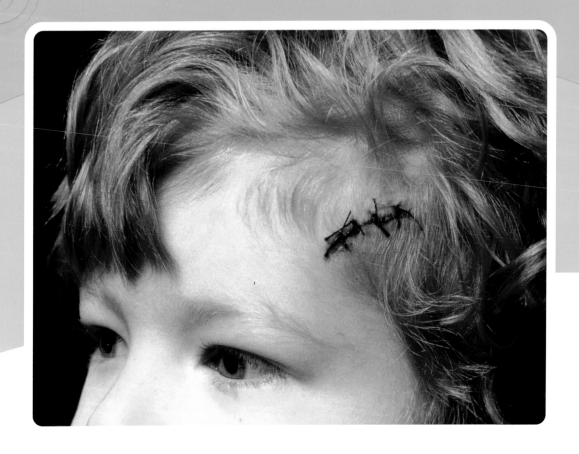

If a cut is deep, a doctor or nurse may have to stitch it. The stitches hold the edges of the **wound** together while the cut heals.

A special thread and a needle are used for stitching a wound. Sometimes special sticky strips may be strong enough to hold the wound.

How a wound heals

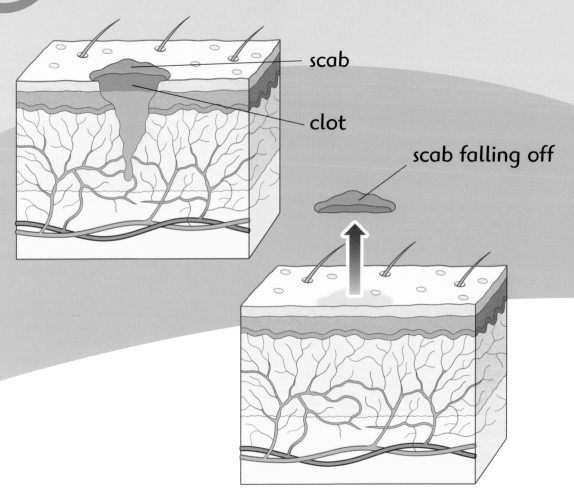

scab

clot

scab falling off

A cut or **graze** heals itself. Blood thickens to form a **clot** over the **wound**. The clot helps to stop the wound bleeding. As the clot dries, it forms a **scab**. A scab is hard and waterproof.

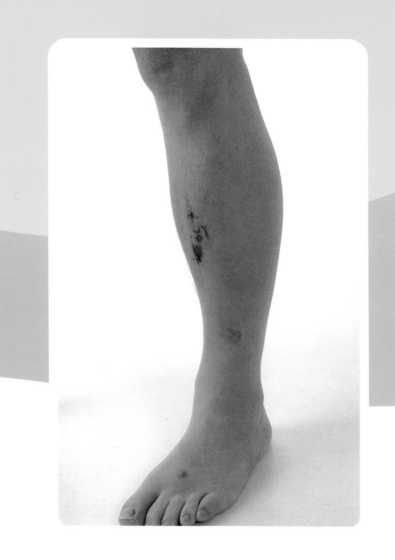

The scab protects the wound while it heals. The broken **capillaries** mend themselves and new skin replaces the damaged skin. The scab falls off once the skin has healed.

Scabs and scars

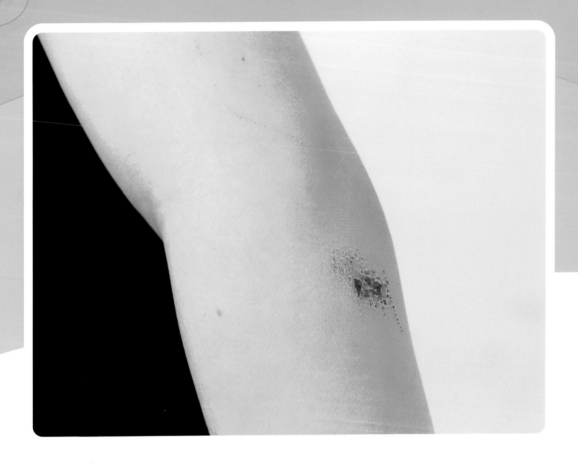

When a **scab** falls off, you can see the new skin below. Let the scab fall off on its own. If you pick a scab off, the cut may start to bleed again and **germs** may get in.

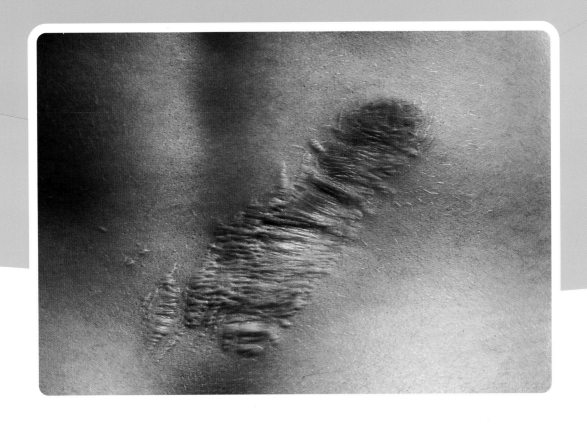

At first the new skin is pinker than the older skin. Some deep **wounds** leave a white mark or **scar** that never goes away.

preventing cuts and grazes

The best way to prevent cuts and **grazes** is to be careful. If you break a glass or bottle, do not pick up the pieces with bare hands.

Ask an adult to cut things with sharp tools for you. Also, when you are in-line skating or skateboarding, wear pads to protect your knees and elbows.

Glossary

accident something that happens by mistake

antiseptic cream cream that contains a substance that stops germs growing in number

balance being able to stand without falling over

bandage long strip of cloth that is used to hold a dressing on a wound

brambles thorny plants that produce juicy, black berries

cacti kinds of plants with spiky stems and no leaves that grow well in deserts

capillaries narrow tubes that carry blood to all parts of the body

clot lump of thick blood

dressing clean pad of cloth that is used to cover wounds

flesh soft muscles and fat that cover your bones

germs tiny living things like bacteria that can cause disease if they get inside your body

graze   a shallow cut area of skin

holly   evergreen plant that produces red berries and has spiky points on its leaves

plaster   small strip of sticky plastic or material that includes a dressing

razor   tool with a sharp blade that is used to shave off unwanted hair

scab   hard crust of dried blood that forms over a wound

scar   mark left on the skin after a wound has healed

wound   cut, graze or other injury to the skin

More books to read

It's My Body: Arms and Hands, Lola Schaefer, (Raintree, 2003)

It's My Body: Legs and Feet, Lola Schaefer, (Raintree, 2003)

Look After Yourself: Get Some Exercise, Angela Royston, (Heinemann Library, 2003)

Safe and Sound: Safety First, Angela Royston, (Heinemann Library, 2001)

Index